Copyright © 2019 by Justin Oberstadt

All rights reserved. No part of this publication may be reproduced, distributed or transmitted in any form or by any means, including photocopying, recording, or other electronic or mechanical methods, without the prior written permission of the publisher, except in the case of brief quotations embodied in critical reviews and certain other noncommercial uses permitted by copyright law. For permission requests, write to the publisher, addressed "Attention: Permissions Coordinator," at the address below.

Village Books
1200 11th St.
Bellingham, WA 98225

Book Layout ©2019 Justin Oberstadt
Cover Design © Sam Dobesh

Ordering Information:
Quantity sales. Special discounts are available on quantity purchases by corporations, associations, and others. For details, contact the "Special Sales Department" at the address above.

Piss and Vinegar / Justin Oberstadt. -- 1st ed.
ISBN 9780578563022

Piss and Vinegar
By Justin Oberstadt

Contents

Intro..3

Love..5

Hate..23

Lost...43

Fight..59

Fate...71

Piss and Vinegar

*Thank you to Mariah Butenschoen, without you
I would have spent all of high school internalizing
all of my teenage angst - and thank you to everyone
that has played a role in my poetry.
No matter if your poem is dark or bright,
you've inspired me to write.*

Introduction

  Poetry is not known for being popular among teenage boys in high school, especially the stereotypical athletic-type. During my junior year at Lynden High, my creative writing teacher, Mariah Butenschoen, assigned several assignments to help hone our class's understanding of figurative language, imagery, and voice. For some reason I still can't deduce, she liked mine. She liked my writing enough that she ended up persuading me to write more - and I did. I was excited, filled with enthusiasm and purpose. I liked being able to write things that, when read, I could watch the emotion on the readers face twist and turn as they navigate through the story I created. The more I wrote, the more I came to realize that poetry is my forte - or so I like to think.

  Once again, I was persuaded by Mrs. Butenschoen to take more of her classes. By the end of my senior year, I amassed over three-hundred poems. Many of which we would go over, critique, and collaborate on - even during the summer. After I graduated, my addiction to writing went rampant. I wrote incessantly, all the while Mariah's email was constantly filled with an absurd amount of poems - (even after school had started again). Thoughts of publishing a book came about, and I loved the idea, but didn't fully expect that it would ever happen...well, here we are.

4

"But what would my poetry book even be about?" I'd ask myself. As I spent more time reviewing my work, a two inch binder overflowing with a few hundred pages of poetry, I realized that my writing had become my way of coping with the struggles I dealt with in high school and life in general. My poetry was nothing like the sweet, blissful poems with soft imagery and cute drawings in the margins. My poetry was raw and bitter, vile and crude. I tried my best to capture the hardest and most painful moments of my life so they might be left on the page rather than sitting patiently in the darkest crevices of my mind waiting to jump out and attack me.

I want my writing to benefit other young men who struggle at home, in school, and in dealing with their most difficult emotions - like I did, not so long ago. To those men, I want to tell you that poetry is not unmasculine. For writers like Sylvia Plath and Charles Bukowski, poetry was savage. It was piercing and filthy. To be able to exorcise your demons through writing, I find that to be a very real kind of emotional strength. Do not neglect your emotions, they are real, and they are powerful - and if you do not keep them in check, they will consume you. To all young men, my wish is that you will find a different perspective on emotional strength through my writing.

Enjoy

- Justin Oberstadt

Love

*Love was by far the hardest emotion to handle
as its counterpart, hate,
can be equally as destructive.*

*As I learned,
even the slightest mistakes in love can be nuclear.*

-the love you don't get back-

you don't get back the love you gave
from the years spent in fruitless relationships
you don't get the love back
from those you cared about most
after they die
you don't get the love back
from those you failed, or gave up on
but somehow
you have to come up with the love
to try again
and to stay alive
love isn't about what you get back
it's about what you put in

-learning the luxury of love-

you will create many things in life
since before you could remember
you created the joy your parents will own
until the day they can't remember anymore
you will go on to create love
as you craft the foundation
on which your relationships will stand
you will write the history books
becoming a part of the days in life
which our children's children will look back on
in amazement and sometimes, grief
you will weave your own thread
through the fabric of time
creating a path every which way you walk
through city streets, and remote woods
inside the trees you carve your name in
or in the paint that you spray on busy buildings
where others see your name, your presence
your threads of fabric intertwine
the food you cook for yourself, and others
will imprint itself on their memories
the taste of chicken noodle soup
you microwaved for a sick friend
on a cold winter day, at home from school
it will forever be the taste of friendship, compassion
and most importantly, love

-A Letter to a Drunken Man-

"You're the most beautiful girl I've ever seen"
You don't fucking know what beauty means.
Beauty is
a friendship blossoming to a vibrant rose.
Beauty is not
a drunken girl falling to the floor,
a sputtering mess of emotions and distress
making meaningless words of the rabbit hole
in her mind.
Beauty is
waking up and pulling her close.
Feeling her gentle heartbeat in your ear,
kissing the warmth of her skin
and knowing she wants to be there.
Beauty is not
a late night flash of loneliness
that spurs into a frantic call of grief
and manifests itself as a woman
on your front door.
Beauty is a night looking up at the stars-
Together.
Finding meaning in the dash of light
only you can see,
shimmering in her eyes.
You see,
you never loved her like I do
She was the stars, the sky, my heart in her eyes,
and nothing
will look at her
like I do.

The following four poems are written across two years detailing the transition between one relationship and the next. And most importantly, growing past the catastrophes they induced.

-I Remember the Night-

Remember how calm and beautiful that night was-
How the lights danced to the rhythm of rumbling.
How can I forget, the love falling from your lips
invaluable moments now, were spent so frivolously.
Do you remember how the lake glistened in the day-
Jealous of the stars that shine in the night.
I am like the lake, looking up to the stars,
as the cracks and howls rise underneath me.
Remember how for a short while I shined?
I thought that I may rest with the stars,
but I can't, for the stars belong to you.
I must lie here upon the breaking ground.
Do you remember when the lights ceased-
And the rumbling lost its rhythm?
You will never know of the quakes,
the quakes that separate your world from mine.
Please, let me see through the eyes of a star-
Do you spectate the brilliance of the galaxy?
Or are you restricted to the blackness of oblivion?
Forgive my curiosity, for I will never truly know.
Forevermore, you will always be with me,
I can never reach you, forevermore.

9

-The Daffodil in the Dark-

Before I could remember the warmth of the sun
I lived and breathed for a hundred years
In the dark of the night.
Until a girl with golden eyes appeared
She bestowed on me a flame, revealing the light
We climbed mighty oaks and powerful pines
Showing each other the endless corners of our lives
Stories we'd tell inspired a thousand to come
But she never told me where she came from
Her light shines bright, it comes from above
I felt the aching in my young heart and mind
I gave her my heart to hold as long as I live
She proclaimed to want nothing but my love
We ventured on, became familiar with our land
Day by day our world would shrink evermore
She would leave to seek comfort in the oceans
While I gather flowers where I'd rest by the shore
The land below the forest lie barren and dead
For I had picked all the flowers in the land
Showing the affection that throbbed in my heart
The golden girl wept for the destruction I had
Her turmoil brought rain and thunder so strong
Lighting brought fire that spreading among trees
I wanted to repair everything that had gone wrong
My madness burned her away with the leaves
The storms and the fire suddenly came to an end
Now I remained alone in my black charcoal world
So my eyes ventured up, to the neglected above
Where I thought I might find my long lost love
Dead flowers covered the dying ashen shore
Eventually I gained the strength to bury them deep
Beneath the earth, where they'd never be found
Until one night I awoke to a beautiful sound
Daffodils grew in the place she took my heart
Glowing a golden hue that reminded me of her eyes
I knew not to pick them, leave them as they are
I would leave these flowers as my reminder in the dark

-After the Quakes-

After the quakes that tore my heart apart
When my entire planet was left in ash
I followed the only beautiful thing in my life
Dazzling stars that glimmered in the night
Every day they'd fade to the blue of the sky
And the sunlight would kill the solace of dark
But when the darkness returns with the stars
I walk to where the stars go to die in the dawn
Path after path, shooting star or falling light
I found the many that mimicked her golden eyes
Broken stars that cannot find their own glimmer
The ones that led me to the dead ends and lies
Venturing the far reaches of my delicate world
Falling out of sanity with every uncertain step
Shattering the hopes and dreams the same way
Similarly to the way the girl with golden eyes did
A ritual lifestyle lived the same way day after day
I broke apart from the skies overbearing sight
Until the earth came still and held its breath
To something that held my fragile world captive
She walked like the world below her was her own
Her eyes spoke of words I had never heard before
Music that sung myself into an immobilizing love
And she like the one before belonged to Pisces
I followed her even through the dark of day
And I dreamed to be her star in the night

-my catalyst-

this is the escapade of love
dancing on the edge of ravines
imagining falling, falling, falling
for everything you've ever dreamed
infatuation consumes you
your mind is caught in the clouds
in the evening of a final sunset
pink, red, and orange
as the colors shine all around
consumed by the walls of infatuation
lips pressed, arms wrapped
eyes gleaming, looking up to the sky
the earthquakes of old rise up
cause tremors and shakes
those of which haven't been felt in ages
molten rock cools on the surface of our skin
her eyes dart from left to right
scanning each individual eye
one at a time
she looks down at my lips for an answer
and repeats
all i see is the world in front of me
a brilliant sight, greater than a starry night
it's a girl, and her eyes, and more importantly
what lies inside
and we can feel it all
the earthquakes of life

At this point in my life, rationalizing each failed romance as catastrophie became an old game. Callousness caused me to begin to finally see the peace within all the chaos of love.

12

-The City, and a Girl-

I found myself in a roaring catastrophe
Intense shuttering, and anxiousness in my eyes
A hundred years lost in the countryside
Helped me forget the sounds of the city
The horrors of the metal beast I forgot hold me
But her gentle grasp on my hand brings me back
Like a tug of war between fiction and reality
All the while, we come closer to the heart
Thrown to the wolves, that prowl the city at night
I can see the sun among the stars in the sky
Perhaps this reality isn't my own, or no one else's
But I know that what's real, is the iron towers
And the warmth of her standing next to me
We found ourselves in good company
Among the fragile pieces of our people's past
Artwork I couldn't fathom in a thousand lifetimes
I fell in awe to the sacred remnants scattered
Gazing deep into the paintings I so loved
You can see the glimmer of creation
Lining each and every stroke of precision
Unfathomable genius spoke like sonnets in my mind
But in this museum of masterpieces
She was the most admirable work of art
And now as I sit here, writing
I almost envy the paintings themselves
A thousand men work to preserve them
The incredible works of art I so admire
And when I think about a life with her
I must achieve the same goal as a thousand men
To preserve ourselves from the detriments of time
To live existentially, and to be remembered
Even if we ourselves, begin to fade away

As I got older, and more mature, metaphors of natural disasters and catastrophe became tiresome. A new love introduced a kind of peace within the chaos- and a new perspective on writing.

-Indecisive, Unimportant, and Regret-

I'd never be anyone's first choice
Nobody would ever see my face
Stranded in a crowd of people
I am not the type to entice
To make a person want to know my name
To listen to my story and maybe
Even give my name
I've never been loved by a girl
The kinds that hold on to you
Through all rationale, for love
It seems the problem is I am easy to forget
Just another stepping stone
Or an old memory to regret
A mistake of the past
Yes, that's all it was, wrong and stupid
Easy to forget

-My Cryptid of the Pacific Northwest-

My ex girlfriend is a Sasquatch
A majestic being of unfathomable beauty
Hidden among the Pacific Northwest
Her mysterious nature lends to curiosity
Of hundreds of men, searching for her
She makes art in the cities quiet coffee shops
You can find them lurking near her home
In the enormous emerald city
And near her quiet little home in the burbs
They all ask, "Is it true? Were you with her?"
Yes, once. I met her long ago
Before the world set out to expose her
Before she was a legend, a myth
Before I lost her, before she was gone
Now she is a distant memory
Grainy photographs and blurry videos
Nobody believes a hoax like me
I am the crazed believer of this girl
I am the Sasquatch man

-When A Man Falls in Love-

Do you know what it's like
For a man to fall in love?
How in a sudden moment
His powerful iron grip on reality
Slips at the sight of an elegant female
Her eyes can derail you
And send you flying through oblivion
Into the brilliant drunkenness of love
And this is the single most frightening thing
For any man to experience
To feel so vulnerable when she looks at you
Tender warming words that soothes
My calloused heart and scar tissue
To fall apart after all that you've been through
And to sleep at night
Without a worry in the world
Because nothing matters more
Than being in love with this girl

-Part two-

But sometimes love fails
A single fight gone too far
Words left unsaid, and nights spent apart
Your bedside turns cold
And soon, so do you

                                                                         -electric-

                                       thunder rolls in the clouds
                           that fog the picture of you in my mind
                   electricity strikes at the touch of your skin
                               and every moment spent with you
                                   is the most fantastic storm
                                      that has ever been

-A Greek Statue-

I remember the night we shared
Lying deep and out under the stars
With the most beautiful work of art
A real masterpiece of flesh and stone
Like the Greek sculptures you see
With beautiful brown eyes
The color of the deep woods
Kissing her put me heart in the sky
I was her lonesome tethered angel
Held down by some rope and promising
A real demon in disguise
At night I dreamed of her, but other things
I dreamed of poison on my lips
Sometimes she could taste it
How the spirits that she tasted
Made her think I cared for other things
I'm a self-made lonely man
A real hopeless romantic
And there's nothing I can do
But to accept the love that the present brings
One day she stopped caring
The love stopped coming
And the stars stopped shining
Love died and we kept on trying
And that was the saddest moment
Remembering the heartlessness in your
Cold stone eyes

The beauty of ancient artwork, from Michaelangelo's David *all the way to Da Vinci's* Mona Lisa *always perplexed me. Everyone just considers these works masterpieces, and if you asked them 'why?' most people could not give you a real answer.*

-Alleys in the Suburbs-

I wonder what happened to my
White wash Angel Wall
It's in an alleyway between two neighborhoods
One that I used to live in
And the other she lives right next to
I wonder who else knows
About the Jesus painted fence
I wonder if fights have happened there
Back where teenagers hide
With cigarettes on their breath
I've shared a kiss with a girl I loved there
Back when the black outlined angel
With a halo looked at us and made it rain
Our lips pressed together like cookie cutter houses
And how we push alleyways in between
I live a hundred miles away now
But she still lives right there
I wonder if our godly graffitied fence remembers me
And how we embraced each other in the rain
Or does it prefer a different memory?
Was this love just not for me?

-What do you think about Love?-

Love is an eruption
When you look into her eyes
Earthquakes and explosions
Inside of your heart and mind
It makes your skin tremble
As you brush together your hands
Love is like molten lava
Gently spilling over my skin
And your hand dances across it
Like forest fires at night
That turn cold when you're gone
Love is a burning passion
For the tingle of sparks on your lips
A jolt of electricity
When I hear her say my name
It's hard to think
I might never hear her say it again

-Screaming-

I could love you with my lips
And I could love you in disguise
Did you ever feel the way my heart moved
When I looked into your eyes
Do you see the past between us
Falling into the darkness between the stars
How it glitters in the light
They almost look like shooting stars
I've always missed you on my birthday
When there are fireworks in the sky
It reminds me of our fantasy
Even when it's not July
You've had my heart since I was young
But we've been apart for many years
There's so many things I want to say to you
But none of them exempt these tears
These words drive me insane
It's become a rabid fear
But I'll scream it every second
I'll even shout it in your face
These words might make you tremble
I want you to hear them, just in case
So I guess here goes nothing
I've thought about this every day
I love you! I LOVE YOU!
It's finally off my chest
Now that it's finally over
Wanna come over
And lay this nostalgia to rest?

-Return to Sender-

A long night ride
And some quiet music to go along
Emptiness inside of the car
Reminds me of the hollowness
Inside my heart
I'm taking a painting back to a girl
My valentine gift, packaged delivery
Mailed back to sender
And I don't expect a reply
Just a kid on a midnight drive
Not a single stop along the way
Just a single destination
A single pair of headlights on the highway
Bringing a girl a stupid painting
One that used to mean so much
I thought I'd always care
But apparently caring wasn't enough

-emptiness-

these days i am intimidated by sleeping in the emptiness of my bed
a twin sized mattress occupied by a single living man
time flies like vultures, or sheep flying overhead
counting down the years, knowing my loneliness might leave me dead

-vulnerability-

you should try to be an alcoholic
so when that beautiful girl dances
like those silly african nomads
shaking and waving their arms
to the beating drum in your heart
you won't have to remember how
horribly vulnerable she made herself
and what disappointment you'll share
when she realizes that you
are not the one

-dead diamonds-

i used to be the one
your hypnotist, your subtle sleeping pill
staring at the view for hours of the year
your mercerizing crowned jewel
finally, a love that felt real
but the sparkle that drew you in
died out like the bonfires we shared every night
until the embers turned to coal
and the diamonds died, just like the midnight sky
i cry out to the hopeless void
a space between the echelons of my heart
and all i hear is the echos
reminding me
that YOU were the one that broke my heart

                                          -relentless adoration-

                                                 your breath on my skin
                                  is a mosaic, a modern day masterpiece
                                      when our lips intertwine, i'm insane
                                            i lose control and abandon peace

-good luck, buddy-

to my ex's next man
her mind is a fortress
an impenetrable storm of fire and rain
she hides her intentions in metaphor
and finding the meaning
may drive you insane
listen to her heart beat
the small quiver in her voice, when she gets mad
it is her soft sung song of silence
And let me tell you,
she was the greatest treasure i never had

-don't forget me-

all it takes is a single day
for the sun to break through the skies
and i promise you
we will watch the world spin around us
a hundred thousand times
we will walk through the forests
as the canopy grows ever so slowly
into the light
the waves will melt on the rocky shores
like the gentle breathing of a happy life
and when the sun sets
the sky will reveal all the brilliant colors
of love
and i promise you
the stars will always shine
even through our darkest nights
so if you might forget me
just look up above
and remember tonight

-it's okay to give up sometimes-

some people you aren't meant to help
no matter how hard you try
no matter what you do
your time and effort
just won't go to use
it's not your fault
and this is true
there are some people
just arent meant for you

-Behind Your Eyes-

There are diamonds in the sky
But only sometimes do they
Remind me of the endlessness in your eyes
Sometimes I can see the time we stayed out
Laughing, crying, talking under the moonlight
How you want to make it big time as an artist
And how you dream of an apartment in the city
I can see blue mornings with the sun rising
Writing poetry about all my insecurities
How they didn't matter to you
Somehow I was still a perfect human being
But lately your eyes just look like
Untouched earth
Hiding the secrets underneath
No matter how much I dig and pry
You'd never tell me what the fuck happened
On that awful, lonely, faithless night
You told me how you were molested
Raped or something along those lines
Some guy mistreated you,
and we both know it wasn't right
Believe me, I'd bash his fucking brains in
If you'd let me unearth his rotten name
I just can't seem to understand
Why I feel like I'm the one to blame

-A Cathartic Experience, or Cardiac Arrest?-

Welcome to the cathartic experience of love
Such a worthless forsaken word
That of tasteless whiskey on my tongue
You forgot the last time you fell head over heels
A once smooth rounded skull
Has now been bashed in at every edge
And nothing of the past seems real
How do you know it all really happened
After your lover is long gone
Who's to tell you the past is true
If every memory feels painful and wrong
Blood dries and scars fade away
But what is left of the memories
Ones you used to make every day
Reckless efforts to keep a love life alive
Kissing any who might have the taste of
Lost love lingering on their lips
Spare me your theatrics, death
I want nothing more than this gift
Give me a woman
Or a rope to hang myself with

I wrote this poem while I was taking an advanced composition class. In the week before our final papers were due we would have brainstorming sessions. My professor made an interesting quote during one of these sessions. Obviously, he couldn't just tell us what to write, so, he would give us just enough "rope" to pull ourselves out of writer's block, or, enough to hang ourselves with. What we did with the information, is our choice.

Hate

If hate were a fuel source, human beings would be the unlimited supply from which the fuel companies would siphon off of.

Sometimes the best way to reflect and move on is to get out of your house, get out of your head, and live a little- to see the world isn't as dark as it is in your mind.

And for me, the best thing I could do was to write.

-Stepping into Adulthood-

If you asked me what's different now
I couldn't tell you.
All I know is the world
Just seemed to get a lot more fucked up
With every damned step I took forward.
I'd stop seeing the ones I loved most
Because commitment became
The most unbearable burden
And all my friends left me at home
When I was in dire need of someone to hold
When you start spending too many nights alone
Pain hangs over your head like a boulder
You can hear the ropes strain to hold it up
Every. Waking. Hour.
I'd spend waiting for it to-
SNAP.
My pain had an unquenchable thirst for alcohol
Like a filthy drunk laying in the streets
I'd see that in my nightmares
Sleeping on cardboard boxes
While my friends slept in warm beds
Laughing and smiling with loved ones
Holding on to their abundance of hope
While I clenched on to old news papers
And cheap beer cans.
But that wouldn't happen...
Would it?

-i'm the archetype-

i'm a passive aggressive, teenage boy
only ever afraid
of other passive aggressive teenage boys
we're like rats in the sewers
found in every plague ridden city street
lacking emotions, and fleeing from our families
and few of us retain heartbeats
we're hate filled hellions cursing brimstone and hellfire
on our failed patriarchal hierarchy
with a disdain for all the pain in life unworthy of living
wishing death to humanity, or just to restart from the beginning

-i was asked why people commit suicide-

if you asked me to describe it
i'd say it's like that lump in your throat
you get when you're sad
that you can't cough, swallow, or relieve
it's name is suicide
and despite what the doctors say
i think it chokes you to death
the black smoke collects in your lungs
and the blankets and pillows smother you at night
until you panic, fighting to relive the attack
but you can't, because it's inside of you.
so you kill yourself, to kill the pain
makes sense right?
it's the only medication a doctor never prescribes
but that's not the end of it
when the air is cleared from your lungs
and your chest sinks into the floor
all your loved ones begin to inhale the noxious fumes
they attract the massive black mass that fills the room
and they begin to die of the same disease
that plagued you
and starts the process all over again
and they'll have to fight, or become consumed

-the burden of a helping hand-

you're lost inside your mind
it's expected, you're going through troubled times
you just don't know what you're searching for
and i mean, that's okay
especially when it's something you'll never find
love and appreciation, belonging and affection
i wish that i could give it to you
but you're stuck inside of depression
and soon i'll be stuck inside of mine

Suicide was a common topic I'd play with- as it plagued me for a long time. But if there's anything I want you to learn from this chapter, its that depression is contagious.

-chaotic nihilist-

i'm not sadistic
i'm a simple minded man
with a .22 caliber machine
a hankering for blood and metal
and lots of stolen diamond rings
torn off the fingers of newly weds
lusting for each other on their
stupidly sacred wedding night
the one they only will ever have
in their dreams
i'm not psychotic
i'm the only person on this earth
that's found out how to be happy
killing time with bullets
and buying love with money and morphine
but you, no no no, you insignificant waste
you crave burning your existence
with putrid nine to five jobs
filling your minds with fabricated realities
the ones you ogle at on the television screen
you're alive so you must consume
and so you stuff your stupid face
so you can sustain the pitiful life you've made
and you work so you can afford to sustain
so you might go on an procreate
over and over again

-midnight-

why must i fantasize
over the fantastic dream
of self-deprecation?
lying on the floor dead
of self induced asphyxiation
what is so wrong
about suicidal contemplation
when i can't even stand
all these therapy conversations

-night time anxieties-

building tension, like cities in my mind
i've got a gun in my hand and i don't know where to go
why must i do this all the time
i shouldn't think like this is the daytime
bank robbery, or suicide, i don't know
i'm building tension, like cities in my mind
i wish i could fit my pain into a single rhyme
it used to never be like this before
why must i do this all the time
i've tried speaking to the gods in the sky
but they don't listen to me anymore
so i'm building tension, like cities in my mind
i run through suburbs and alleyways at night
running away from corpses in the grocery store
why do i do this every time
nobody is dead, i'm in my bed, lying
but i can't solve this conflict
i don't know what's wrong
i build tension, like cities in my mind
why do i do this all the time

-the tool-

i may be a tool
but at least i'm getting used
you're lying in the corner
i'm preferred between me and you
i may be broken and abused
but at least i've become used to it
i've got nothing left to lose
but at least i'm making use of it
you see, when you're like me
nothing can be felt at all
they'll drive you up the wall
you're insignificant and small
i'd rather feel this rotten love of self loathing
than to pretend i'm not loved at all

-Those Past-

At the dawn of a new night
We're a single grain of sand
Standing up to a tsunami
Holding anxiety in our hands
At the end of the day
We're garbage in the ocean
Just, floating on alone
Our mothers and fathers die
Funerals of Walmart trash bags
And a cardboard casket
Everything that's left of them
Turns to worthless memories
Our sisters and brothers fade away
And we find ourselves at home
Haunted by these entities
Even in the day
Where did the time go?
Is there a discount on the past?
Just yesterday I was twelve years old
Crying at the grocery store
Begging for a treat
And now
Friends are broken souls
Or a ghost of who they used to be
I hate this pretend reality
Let me go to the past
Where sunsets were still beautiful
When love felt like fireworks
On the Fourth of July
Now I just want to die
Lonely and broken
In a lonesome empty field
Kill me now and I'll forget
What the past used to be

Hate is not always outwardly expressed. Sometimes, the most hateful people I've ever met were fanatics of hating themselves.

-what is depression-

depression
its writing in all lowercase letters
because words won't make a difference
its laying in bed exhausted
but never being able to fall asleep
wondering what it was that made you
into a worthless bag of skin and bone
wondering doesn't scratch the surface
why you didn't have the strength
to fathom what you had
not being able to say "it's over"
or "they're gone"
depression is a black and white filter
of novocaine and nyquil
numbing the emotions
so you cut them into your skin
depression
is not being able
to come to
the en-

-critique-

their kind eyes
speak foul lies
ones i can barely
stomach to hear
my anxieties fuel me
a furious gasoline
with no wheel to steer
i'm not so talented as i think i am
and i'm not so clever, i fear
i believe i am
a worthless man
so don't flatter me, my dear

30

-sitting alone in an empty parking lot at two a.m.-

i'm in love with sober, self loathing, me
that man that walks
with a thousand yard stare
darting aimlessly into the dark
without a whim nor dare
he tells me i'm healthy
but drunk me can't compare
sober self loathing justin is reckless
he drives cars aggressively hoping to crash
he burns metal into my calloused skin
he severs relationships for sake of self
to get back at the version of me
that doesn't want to give in
self loathing sober justin is a man I fear
he doesn't cry, he doesn't die
he doesnt live, he doesn't breath
he'll walk over cliffs, he'll suffocate me
all for the enjoyment
of eradicating my beliefs
he can't be fucked with
he's vengeful, and conniving
i know he wants to kill me
and i cant keep surviving
when the man my family
tells me i need to be
is the one who wants
to eradicate me

One of the hardest things to realize; you are not <u>you</u> when you're intoxicated. You are who you are in your most vulnerable moments.

-What is Suicide-

Suicide is
The taste of cold steel
Only speaking in vowels
With a pistol pressed to your cheeks
Suicide is hatred for the world
A distaste for society and yourself
One that can't be numbed with
The bitter taste of alcohol or drugs
Suicide is a selfish act
One that betrays the love of many
For the relief of an indescribable pain
Suicide is a constantly throbbing thorn
Stuck in the darkest caverns of your soul
Festering and swelling
With the vile fluids of depression
Ones that paint the ceiling red
With the colorful brains
Of the living dead

-Self Induced Depression-

My life is one of hatred and violence. I want to kill my memories and burn the bridges I used to cross. You don't belong here, truly, you will not find a heart to mend, nor will you find someone to hold and pretend- to pretend that love is something real. To pretend that it's sweet aroma lasts longer than the taste of whiskey on your lips. There's nothing here for you. I've spent years trying to make something out of nothing and all I've come up with is broken promises and enemies. I'd kill myself but my hands aren't made for killing. They're made for writing. They're made for holding. You could kill me- and if only you would.

32

-From the Lips of a Poet-

You'll hear many words
Ones that taste like vinegar
And some that smell like roses
You will spit foul phrases
And you will hear elegant melodies
Spilling from the lips of deceit
But not all is as it seems
I can make a hate speech
Taste like fresh apple pie
I can turn a pretty poem
Into a horrible nightmare
One that'll make you scream
I can make a brave speech
Become a pile of divorce paperwork
Or perhaps a declaration of war
You see, I am a poet
My tongue looks like gold
But tastes like bile and bleach
I am a sour reminder to the world
That not is all as it seems
Words are malleable
And have the ability to bend or break
Under the influence of love
Or under tension of hate

Honestly, I hate calling myself a poet. Everyone has some kind of guard to hide their emotions, and to me I guard myself by use of metaphor. I hide the most painful memories I have in poetry because poetry is often times subjective, so the only person that truly knows what a poem about, is me- meanwhile I get to watch people try and interpret my poetry. In this way I'm able to get away with sharing my feelings, without really exposing myself.

-Cocktail of Disdain-

The world doesn't know me
The world doesn't love me
The world doesn't care
Nothing like a double dose of self loathing and jealousy
To formulate a concoction of disaster to undo me
The same one that'd tear my life apart
This world is worse
Than the one I went to bed in the past day
Nothing like the end of the humanity
And fulfillment of life itself
To make me hate the sunrise, and the birds
People see you as another object
Another easy one night stand
Another person to walk over
Walking through the human wasteland
Leave me out of all the petty emotions we all feel
They're the chasers to an alcoholic drink
One I'd hack down my throat
Give me a quick death and a meaningless life
Before I have time
To think about what could've been
I don't care about the pain
Nothing is as great a threat as my emotions
Something I'd rather have out of the way

-Pull the Pin, I dare you-

I'm what you never want to find
Someone that will ruin you
Beyond hopeless repair
Give it time...
And I'll desolate you
With my destructive serenade
I'm a crater that has yet to reveal
Baby, I'm your fragile hand grenade
All yours to hold, till death do us part
I'm warm to the touch,
A compact disaster
Ready to detonate inside your hands
Release me into oblivion
Or allow me to demolish anything and everything
You have ever come to love
I wish I could help myself
I wish I was just a dud
That my love wasn't this destructive
But then again, who has time for fateless love

Some inspiration from the movie 'The Fault in our Stars'; it seems sick, and painful to call yourself a grenade, or a ticking time bomb. But in a way, its true- only so long as you think you will hurt everyone in your life, you will. But if you live each moment living in fear, you never really will live.

-A Nightmare-

I taste the blood in my mouth
And all I see it metal
The cages, the chain link fences, and barbed wire
The crowds chant hatred and violence in tongues
And there is a feral animal inside of me
Growling with my throat
Clawing with my nails
Biting with my teeth
I used to be someone else
But what's left of me
Is left in vomit on the pavement floor
I don't know who they are, or why I'm here
But I know I want to kill them
To rip the guts out from their gizzards
To hear the flesh tear from their bones
To hear their bones grind and crack
Under my cold lifeless hands
I want to feel the warmth of their blood on mine
To feel it cover me, and dry on my skin
As it morphs me into something else
I'm not who you think I am
I don't know me anymore
I don't care if you kill me now
Because like them
All we are,
Is blood and guts on the pavement floor

*Many of my poems I'd write frantically as soon as I'd wake up.
Nightmares and dreams were the source of many poems, and if I didn't
write them thoroughly, they'd be lost to my subconscious.*

-Dismemberment-

Cut open my chest
Tear apart the flesh
And you won't find a heart
You'll find some lungs
Full of smoke
And a frog
In my throat
Something that you've got to blame
Watch the blood pour
From my veins
You'll find nothing but hate
In their grotesque, disturbed,
meticulous state
Saw into my brain
You'll find memories
Washed away
But you'll find
That my love for you
Looks the same
Snap off my fingers
Like branches
Of the trees
we used to climb
They should never have
Been yours to hold
Listen to my spine
Cracking
Over every stair
Listen to yours
Is it even there?
There's blisters
On my swollen knees
Bending over backwards
And rolling
In agony
And sometimes
We just don't feel
The same

Living in Washington state, winter was a large part of my daily life. Gray clouds overhead every waking hour, sunrise and sunset nearly six to eight hours apart, you begin to get a surreal sense of reality. Some days you don't want to wake up knowing the day will be over before it's begun.

-Winter-

I can feel it
Time is stagnant
And the sun is lost behind the clouds
That separates us from our former reality
And ourselves
Sometimes I dream of the heavens
But I am awoken to the sound of thunder
That overbearing storm in my mind
Sometimes I think it will break me
The ominous clouds weigh me down
Or those that stand to kill me
Yet, I remain unbroken
There is but only one option
Bide your time
Wait for the sun to find itself again
And pray that the end of the world
Doesn't come crashing down on you
In this nightmare
Wait until life can be free again.

But listen once more,
You may live, and you may survive the storm
But year after year
It will come for you
Like death, it is immortal
One day it will break you
And death will find you
And bring you
Back to me

-The Witching Hour-

Winter comes fast, falling to the darkest dawn
We draw our eyes towards its last glimmer
Of gracious golden light clinging onto the air
As it falls behind the horizon until it is gone

Frost is not the only visitor brought so subtly
In the dead of night, they crawl under your skin
They have no need for a name, but only a voice
Whispering forbidden words of unfathomable sin

Their taste is singular, the color of the white snow
Falling heavy over the blackened pine trees
Warmth of blood, rushing over your cold body
And the taste of flesh rotting in an open grave

We find ourselves open to often, to these beasts
In the witching hour of such ungodly winter nights
Perhaps we should shut ourselves from the cold
And seek to kill all the demons inside

Knowing we live with them, these demons to be
Somewhere locked away from the summer nights
You've been neglectful, you know the sun will die
You're stuck in this hell, you don't even know why

Perhaps their inside all of us, and we're all fiends
But then again, maybe the only demon is me?

Bullying, abuse, and victimization are things many western countries seem to normalize. But it's not normal, and for many it's the only world they know. You see it all over, from videos on the internet, to your daily life. But not everyone takes it home with them, and struggles with it.

-Between Worlds-

You've seen this all before
In videos on the internet
Kids that couldn't know any better
Maybe so subtly, it doesn't catch your eye
Bruises seem to hide so easily
Even if you find a way behind the lie

You notice them walking past you
Neglect has a sound you can't quite hear
And the taste of blood still hurts
But you lack the knowledge
And they lack the confidence
To voice the hurt that stings bleeds

Even when the day comes
When they can finally take a moment to breathe
When the voice of resistance breaks free
Words like "boys will be boys"
Almost hits harder than they do
And they find themselves evermore alone

So that creeping thought starts to make sense
A dark familiar voice speaking the only sense
A voice of redemption, and freedom
Whispering of a world
Where everyone misses them
And wished that something had changed
A world without constant heartache
Somewhere to rest for forever

So the last voice they can trust is their own
And even that one starts to turn against them too

-Too Quiet-

There it is again
The rage in my words, and mind
I hate it- all this
I know it's in there, the beautiful machinations of my mind
Caressing memories of the past
Like a gentle spirit, soothing to remind
Sometimes they fall out, like a gentle river in your mind
But not all are gentle, and kind
Some are dark and powerful- like a winter storm
They've got ideas of their own
And these- they roar like a tornado in your home
Sometimes you can hear them talking to each other
Schizophrenia is the sound of the gears in my head
And now- they are killing me from the inside out

-Poetry Scat-

Your demons laugh upon you with your feeble attempts to run
They've memorized every crevice, every item under the sun
Power, Love, and Justice are the only three ways to die
Power grants you a false immortality, strength is only a lie
Love gives you a peaceful death, but walks hand in hand with grief
Justice is when you accept your fate, greeting death with a sigh of relief

-Intuition-

Rage courses through my veins
The heavy blood strengthens my body
But it distorts my mind with a fiery blaze
I will bash in his skull with a single blow

Coursing veins pulsing with my heart
Propel my fists into everything
Uncontrolled, explosive fury
Leaves my surroundings desolate

Hate fills my being like boiling water
I am drowning with no lungs
I scream ruthlessly at the water
The fire inside of me is extinguished

I am drowned, surrounded by my captor
Motionless, boiling water turns cold

That blank stare is a banner for emotional vacancy
I'm not hurting, I'm just not here right now
It's like looking for light between the stars
Verbally battering me only darkens the sky

Do you see the imaginary gun pointed to my head
It fires imaginary bullets with every interaction
Dead eyes don't see the stars in the sky
Their sight is limited to deaths hollowed reach

I can't tell if when I'm predicting my own future
If my predictions birthed from emotional upsets
Or if they are destined, and I am wise
Or if my predictions become destined
Because of my preconceived idea
That my predictions are all I have

-inception-

my mind fills the space in an empty room
i spill my anxieties all over the floor
covering the carpet with a billion intricacies
and for a moment i am standing above the echelons of space
i hear a voice, and then a thousand
whispering under their breaths
screaming at the top of their lungs
and begging for an answer
that i do not have
my conscience is struggling to grasp his own concept of reality
leaving me with an empty care
i reach out into nothingness
and end up throwing myself into orbit
with a sun just moments from supernova
the windows shatter on impact
sending shards of glass
like floating space dust
penetrating my vital organs
i shed a thousand tears as i spill my guts into your galaxy
soon, my fossilized body fluids will fuel a conquest
to learn, to control, and understand what i never could
they'll go on to stand at the golden gate
as they bask in the triumphant glory of their feat
until the moment they find that on the other side
is just another room

Have you ever had intensely deep conversations with someone, just to arrive at the end not really having learned anything at all? Yeah, that's what this poem is about.

No, I'm not kidding.

Yes, it is kind of stupid. But so are falsely deep conversations.

Lost

*Being lost is a part of life, and despite its abrasiveness,
being lost has the ability to lead you to exactly where you need to go.
Eventually, you find yourself, years later, a completely different person
living in a seemingly different world. For better, or for worse.*

-king of solitude-

if i never find love
i think that it might be because
i am an uncompromising asshole
or maybe, a naive, two faced prick
the guy with a knack for unfaithfulness
and sometimes, i mean, i can be a dick
at times i'm worthless, stupid
a guy just can't get a break
what a half-hearted man, they say
i hang my head low, for others' sake
"who could love a face like that"
a mother who's income is child support payments
"what's wrong? be a man! cat got your tongue?"
"don't you know you're supposed to help others-
when you can tell something's wrong?"
what about me?
i'd be able if i wasn't alone for so long.
maybe someone would love me
if i never made a mistake, or maybe if I was rich
maybe if my body was perfect
and i had a bigger dick
maybe then i'd deserve it, maybe then i'd be loved
maybe it's God who's torturing me
watching me squirm from above...
weekends, holidays, i lay awake at night
pondering the question
if she ever comes, will i know it's right?
or will i pass her by, will i wish i had tried?
shut it out, break away all naïveté
for loneliness is my kingdom
and solitude, i am it's king.

-the ocean made me think of this one-

i'm prepared for a tidal wave
the tsunami that lies just at my feet
towering walls of water
ready to come down on me
i've always known it was coming
no hiding, or running, not this time
not anymore
no miracles, no rescue, no flying
i don't fear dying, because i've done this before
don't cry if i wind up as lifeless
a cold corpse up on the pacific shores
just remember that i went down fighting
and giving up wasn't my option anymore

-graduation-

the cheap graduation gowns
are made of a disappointing stale polyester
and they wrap extra fabric around your neck
to signify that you did better
i like to imagine the successful kids
got the fabric caught on a loose wire
or stray hook
and then their own achievement
would strangle them
the same way my disappointment
strangles me

-What is Loneliness-

Loneliness is an empty road
A thousand miles of the past behind you
And an infinite sea of nothingness ahead
Walking is the only choice you have
Backwards is your safest bet
But what if you go forward instead?
Loneliness is staying awake at night
Coming home to have nothing to do
Lying around the house
Wishing there was someone to talk to
Praying you might be invited
To spend a night out on the town
With all the friends from the past
But every time you check your phone
You're just let down
Loneliness is being quiet for too long
Wishing you could open your mouth
To share the endless thoughts
To spill pure emotion from your lips
To explode with excitement in the best way
And to see the expression on the faces
Of people that care about what you're saying
But there's no one to say these things to
There's no one to hear a word
It's an endless isolation ahead of you
So for now, you go unheard

Justin,
It's either
I feel too much
Or I feel too little
I can't write
Because
I just don't feel anything
Reading and reading,
Trying to get anywhere
NEAR emotion
And to avoid the truth
I can't ever see myself
Feeling passionately enough
To connect with other people
I've got assignments due tomorrow
And an important interview
But instead
I'm sitting here
Silently reading poetry to myself
Because- other than you
It's the only thing in this world
That makes me feel
Just a little, less empty lately
Justin, I really hope you don't read this
I'm sorry I waste your time-
Sometimes
And that I can't hear clearly
And that I say stupid things
And that I talk too much
Without ever saying anything at all
Fuck this
All I ever wanted to do
Was sleep
But I just
Fucking
Can't
One time
I slept through a fire alarm
Remember when you got stuck in the snow?
I wasn't there to be awake with you
And that scares me
So much
How does a person even do that
I don't know anymore
How many times I've had to
stay awake
To make sure people stay sane
Through the night
Or even just being there
When their parents kick them out
One time,
I ran out into the forest, calling her name
In the dead of night
Eventually, there she was
Lying on the forest floor
Laying under a pine tree
Soaking wet from the rain
Next to her
An empty orange pill bottle
Every ounce of weight fell from my head
And my heart sank
To the forest floor
With her
And maybe that's why
I've lost so much feeling over the years
Spending all my time
Pouring my heart out
To other people
It's all bullshit really
Because they just end up using you
And you let them
But I still
Can't
Sleep

-A.B. ; 2017

Unlike any other poem in this book, I did not entirely write this one. Poetry comes from intense emotion, laced in metaphor, or twisted by word play. This poem was a series of texts sent to me. All I did was a few small edits.

-I wish I didn't write-

This isn't poetry
Words aren't meant for these
Malformed memories
I was only eleven years alive
Blaring out the sounds of
A brutal divorce
Outside my bedroom door
The ugly reality of it is
I cried until my face was numb
Until tears left a trail in my skin
Wet and red like the rivers of Babylon
Where I sat remembering Zion
And I never did a thing about it
Nobody ever took a bullet
Dad never walked out on us
My mom didn't succumb to drugs
And my siblings aren't mental
But look at us now
Do we look like a success story?
There wasn't a great tragedy
That I could write about in great detail
Our tragedy was never having one
To fade away like dust in the wind
A lot of pain and suffering
What for? Nothing.
So when you tell me, this is a poem
I want you to know that this is my tragedy
You wouldn't know about it
Unless I said it

-Finally, a Beautiful Dream-

Roses in the winter
Aren't the only thing that's bitter
When the sun doesn't shine
No, never.
Not quite long enough
In the golden, numbing sky
When the snow fell I dreamed
I was outside of our home, listening
To all our subtle quiet screams
And the way
They'd twist and bend
In the frozen winter wind
Roses aren't the only ones that die
When the heaviest clouds
Make their way across the skies
along with those
wilted scarlet petals.
We all know that love dies
I dreamed,
That in the midst of incoherence
It can't be spoken, but you hear it
The love and fear
The death of love
That I couldn't bare to hear
In the broken, sobbing, and screams
And so I dreamed.

-Rooftops-

Funny how much I found in this small town
A skateboard, a life, and a friend or two
But it wasn't always a fantastic paradise
I was born into this city with hatred, and loneliness
At first the rooftops were a place to go to die
I'd sit above, staring at my hellish grave below
The moon did not shine on me for some time
I was stuck sleeping in the ditches by the road
I'd skate through the empty streets alone
Looking for someone that liked the night
But I'm just another kid with worn out vans
Sick with boredom and disdain
But to my bewilderment,
I found others that liked the night and torn jeans
Blasting music and knocking over neighbors trash cans
We climbed the rooftops and rolled down them
As we stand as kings above our garbage world
But before our time here has ended
You're long gone, and you don't even know it
So now I sit above the ground in fishing nets
Telling strangers our story of the rebellion and vice
But they'll never know what it was like
Being a mishap, and alone
And making use of the time you had
Sitting on the rooftops, alone

This poem is a reflection of my time spent adjusting to living in a new place. Dealing with step-parents and trouble at school, I began spending my nights on rooftops.

-pyro-

i can no longer find my own heart
there is a gaping hole in my chest
but i can feel it
it is lost in a distant land
surrounded by faceless people
in such a fragile paper town I lived in
the same ones I used to love
it is in these paper towns
in towns made of paper
it is dangerous to hold a match
do you know what it's like?
to set fire to your own world
against your own free will
and to be forced to watch it burn
shrinking away as it falls apart

-Thermochemistry-

Life burns with beauty on the coldest days
Crystals of winters white covers our surroundings
Our love could not keep us warm for this long
Oh, how the low winter sun burns on my skin
Life chills to the bone even in the warmest nights
Sitting by the fire without a single one to love
Gentle caress of the lake doesn't soothe my pain
Oh, but the moonlight was always my favorite
Showing me what I could never show you alone
How the stars were my guide all this time
You're long gone now, and you don't even know it
A distant memory on my unlit Christmas tree
Another face on an ornament I can't explain
My family can find me so far away, in the city
Telling strangers our story of the sun and moon
My body is warm by the fire, but my heart is frost bitten
I'd give it all away, your forsaken gifts
Perhaps to someone that will love like I do

52

-I Wrote Poetry (instead of enjoying a party with friends)-

There's those nights our parents will never hear
All the emotions and decisions they'll never see
But we'd spill it all out to the first kid
that we thought would understand how we felt.
I know what it's like to lose your senses
Sacrificing the night to forget about the rest
Your mind slips away like the summer days
And you find yourself fading away into the night
I know what it's like to live with a lot of pain
Tears sting your face after falling too long
The time slows by the day as we depress
And it all turns to gray because of the stress
I've been writing, thinking, crying, being wrong
And I don't know if I can hold on for long
I'm sure there's something behind this all.
The purpose, a meaning, or maybe something else
But maybe I'm the only one, dying in the night
And if not I can't find reason to save myself
After all these damned nine to five days
Killing the child that loves to create and love
I can feel myself fading into darker days

-indecision-

i'd never commit suicide
but if i did
it wouldn't be in my home
i'd be a hundred miles away
on a mountain top, alone
i couldn't hang myself
it'd be with a bullet and a gun
quick and painless
like the movies show
i'd slip off at night, quietly
and not leave a note
so they never see inside of me
not even inside my skull
they'd never see all the problems
that i made believe my fault
but then again none of this matters
because i won't

-Sincerely-

I never wrote a letter in my life
And now they tell me that I'm gonna die
I'll have to reach you through the afterlife

Tell me about those minutes after I left
How you cried tears of tidal waves all night
I never wrote you a letter in my life

You broke me among the stars in the sky
I found the words to say only after I had died
I'll have to reach you through the afterlife

The moon didn't provide an ounce of solace
I couldn't find the will to write the words I felt
I would never write you a letter in my life

The letters I wrote were never addressed
I handed them to you while my heart still beat
I'll have to reach you through the afterlife

It kills me now, that I am writing on this day
Because you are dead and so am I
I never wrote a letter in my life
I'll have to reach you through the afterlife

My Dad bought me a book when I graduated high school called A Little Book on Form. *This book was a huge source of expanding what I already knew about poetry. The poem above is one of my experiments with a Villanelle- a type of French poem.*

-My Mistake-

I'm what you find in the filthy city streets
The black tar that seeps into the sewage
When the rain soaks into my silt skin
I'm the infectious waste your parents warned you about as a kid

I've ruined many people. For reasons I can't explain

What can burn brighter than the sun
And tear a hole through my rotten chest
Something that takes everything from you
And leaves me with all the rest

What kills you when the sun goes down
And rots your beating heart all the way through
It suffocates the person you were months ago
Now I hate myself so you don't have to

What leaves you feeling broken and devastated
The end of the world wouldn't feel nearly as bad
From now on you'll never see the world the same
The fact that I changed you isn't nearly as sad

Do you think you're the first one to feel this?
From the dawn of age, to Shakespeare's lovers
To the pathetic excuses of adolescence today
There's been heartbreaks before you by the hundreds

I love you, and there's never a doubt within me
I just can't find the people we used to be

-Suburban Nightmare-

We're the kin of rebellion and daring innocence
Riding bikes under the protection of the night
Laughing and crying from within the sleeping city
Like a dream it's forgotten as the sky turns bright

Breaking laws and tree branches under our own free will
Fleeing from the conformity of an oppressive home
We are the monsters in the night that were never real
And we break the powerful silence of night- alone

We overstayed our welcome in God's frigid night
Our bikes were overtaken and destroyed by your life
And the man in robes tells of the end of my excursions
To the hell of metal wrists, and a concrete afterlife

I ran from the man in robes that intended to kill
Howling at me- and locking buckshot into a chamber
Hellhounds snapped at my feet climbing over walls
I hear a gunshot and impact- tasting fear as a flavor

I'll run forever until I become tired of running
Or until the robed man finally shoots me dead
Whatever happens the darkness of night will live on
Let my fear guide me so I may shoot myself in the head

Ride on you rebellious souls- into the frigid night
Before you're dead, or overtaken by the light

-Emptiness-

I'm drifting through this lake
My heart echoes in black mountains
There is a rumble that shakes me
That violently ruptures my past

I follow these vibrations
Like an omen calling out to me
Knowing well what is out there
And what awaits me in the dark

Beneath me is a million miles
Of quiet, motionless glass
Clear enough to see through
But dark enough to see the past

The pine trees whisper quietly
Under protection of the night
Talking to the predators
That are hiding from the light

Valley after valley
I cross the horizon like a sea
There's something out there watching
And I don't think it's the trees

I've found no trace of what it is
No tracks, no scent, no trace
Whatever it is, is lifeless
But I can always feel its gaze

-I think I'm dumb-

As a pupil to my planets natural course of action
I've been told everything happens
Along a specific course of action
And reaction
I was told that someone
Has to take the role of a villain
I just never thought it would be me
But I've never enjoyed the killing

I lived in a family full of love
But I never felt a belonging
Running off into the horizon
I'd dream of the ocean singing

Blood dripping from my wounds
Coming home only to repeat
They'd hear me healing my pain
But my entire family stayed asleep

I've never even thought of murder
I couldn't hurt another human being
She crashes and throbs behind my head
I begin to kill myself when the ocean sings

Her tides roll out and I see what's inside
The vermin that crawl beneath my skin
Suddenly everything right seems wrong
But I know my heart lies further out within

Every so often my wounds bleed too much
I sing out to her from over the horizon
Where her silence is a beckoning anger
It shakes me with a violence that begins rising

Burning the walls of my families home
I always end up killing myself when I'm alone

-ignorance is bliss-

we were all once just kids on the playground
enjoying the sunshine, squealing around
mothers watched from a distance
conversating quietly, as to alert to any dangerous sounds
but what these parents don't know
is that as these children grow
it's not the rapists or stranglers
that will snuff out a peaceful life
where they might survive and growing old
it's neglect and abuse from too few words said
when they needed it most
i can't tell you how many nights i was left alone
listening to my parents tearing apart our nice home
as divorce ravaged my brother and sister and i
all these parents keep us sheltered with lies
cause they don't want us to see the real world
we all know what happens to the boys and girls
who learned too much, too fast
they lived too long with a fucked past
and never dealt with the demons inside
it's not like we're born to be drug dealers and stabbers
it's casual drinking, and smoking that develops drug habits
it's loneliness and rejection
that creates kid killers that you can't fathom
so what's to blame for all of this?
is it neglectful parents, stubborn kids, or the evil doers doing this?
i say, it's the blindness of our ignorance
yeah sure, ignoring reality is bliss

Fight

After all the suffering and melancholy you will experience in your life
you have to decide- will I run from my emotions and experiences?
Or will I fight to preserve everything I stand for, and everything I want to be.
For many, it takes unrelenting fury and ambition to fight in the face of opposition.

Some might say, you're full of Piss and Vinegar.

-the infinite war-

my bones ache
and my muscles are sore
from the days i've spent
fighting my war
the faint light of the rising sun
softly soothes this heavy heart in my chest
so i take my seat on the mountain top
for my final rest
my demons are slain
and i've made my peace
but i know it won't last
not forever, at least
do not fear, my friends
remember my struggle
and how hard i fought
remember your pain
and the perseverance i taught
for the darkness inside you
it can never be killed
but without the eternal struggle
your life will never be fulfilled
fight every battle
with all of your vigor, and might
never lose hope, as close as you might
and always remember
this is not the final fight

The end of one thing only means the beginning of something new. So when you have the chance, rest. And no, this poem does not have any affiliation with the movie- <u>or does it</u>?

-Not an Excuse, just an Explanation-

No matter how hateful, bigoted, or mistreated
Even the worst of us still have a heartbeat
I've seen people murder animals for the adrenaline
And I've seen passionate men and women
Turn soulless and obsolete
I've heard screaming, and fighting
I've watched cursing, and dying
All for them to arrive at an inevitable suicide
Or worse- a hateful life
But no matter the evil I've seen
I know we're all decent people, all of us- human beings
Perfect minds, we're born
A clean slate, ethereal, and blue
But the trust and love of a newborn's eyes
Can be betrayed to, and lied
Their minds grow disfigured, as they forget the truth
The loving touch of a familiar family member
The respect and loyalty of a forever friend
Due to a lack of love in a life they knew
They live on into adult life, and pretend
All those cozy emotions were a fallacy
An empty promise of an unforgiving earth
Sometime we must forget how alone we are
And remember to sometimes put others first
Because that loneliness and hatred
Can fester in your mind
Twist you rotten, and make you blind
But try to take someone out of it
Even just for a day
Remind them the sun is shining
And that you love them
Because truly, we're all the same.

-Learning to Swim-

When the water rises
And every man and woman stands reaching their necks
To try and gasp at a single breath of fresh air
You must learn to thrive
As you claw, and grasp, and fight to breathe
That is what must come, before you learn to float
Before the water fills your lungs and throat
By any means necessary
You must enthrall yourself in the struggle
To sink or swim, or to drown and die
Rather than to survive and work, but to live and create
You must fight, to survive
You must create to stay alive
By any means necessary
You must strive to become the catalyst of self-preservation
To breathe life back into the world from whence you came
And to lift others from their inevitable fate
Because, at the end of the day
We all choke and die
But it is better to be living
Than to be kept alive

-joker-

it's going to be okay
because one day
the problems of tomorrow
will be nothing but
silly mistakes
the things we make fun of
a self-deprecating comedy
of yesterday

-Forrest Gump-

Feathers in the sky
Floating down, down, down
All the way to the horizon
They speak of secrets
As the sun sets, dying
Speaking softly of a storm
I never listen, but I'm trying
The next morning
Heavy rain clouds hover
As everyone runs for cover
All my roots rise up
And hold on tightly to my feet
I guess again,
The rain must wash right over me
My fateful fertilizer
Making me turn over a new leaf
The clouds will fade
As the sun rises once again
This time I'm stronger
No longer dying in the shade

64

-you never know how close you really are 'til you're there-

there is still air in your lungs
no matter the smoke, you may choke
but you'll never forget how to breathe
there is still blood in your heart
and as long as you keep moving
it still beats
there is still a world inside your mind
you may think it's lost
but there's still time
because everything you want
might only be one breath
one thought
or one heartbeat away

-'The Road' is one of my favorite movies-

you've walked this road for so long
you're headstrong, but your will's weak
your knees begin to buckle
and you back starts to ache
the beginning is so far behind you
but death stands right beside your feet
please, just take another step
put your hand right here, for me
do you feel the heartbeat in your chest?
it means you've still got fight in you
so long as it still beats
the mountains tower above you
and anxiety lies within
depression fills the rain clouds
and you think back to where you've been
the sunny, grassy meadows
the forests, green and lush with life
now all you know is suffering
pain and sacrifice
but remember you are stronger
you're the titan of this earth
and the world that wants to kill you
is the same one that gave you birth

-what is a soul-

i like to think of a soul
as an ethereal blanket
born white, soft, and pure
like a baby's blue eyes
but as life goes on we stain
dragged through the filth of the streets
and we blemish from the stresses
that, naturally, come with each day
and we tear, from heartbreak, and loss
but you can be cleansed
and sown together again
by watching the sun rise over the mountains
you can go to church and give yourself to god
but falling in love is my personal favorite
all things that create you, make you new
and in the end, the wears, the tears
the pains and the stains
make you
you

Religion is something I've struggled with throughout my life. The idea of an afterlife, heaven and hell, I don't know. But I can say this, if a soul does exist, it is malleable, can be cleansed, and is never too far gone.

-dante-

we've come far since rock bottom
you've broken bones hitting bedrock
but we've never nearly forgotten
what it was like being dead locked
we've been trapped in this changing maze
our labyrinth of fear and doubt
we made habits setting our souls ablaze
cause we can't find our way out
but life has never been hopeless
dante still saw the golden gates
and he told us:
the angels are as close to hell
as satan is close to heaven
as hope is to yourself
so keep climbing, keep digging, keep crawling
until your fingernails bleed and tear
until your shattered and broken and scarred
until you've torn out all your hair
life is pain, we're meant to suffer and doubt
but i promise you'll get there
i promise you'll find your way out
life is a journey, it has its ups and downs
earth, heaven, hell, and everything all around

-more water metaphors-

when the water washes over me,
it comes in waves.
powerful lapses of weight thrown down
so hard it sometimes knocks me out
my torn skin stings from the saltwater
and every movement to get back up
is memory and pain of the wounds that falling left behind on my
stone cold skin
one day the pain might make my eyes roll back
and my skin will turn soft and gray
the ocean will reclaim me
and my body will decay
all that will remain is a dead spot in the sea
where a stubborn man took a stand
and somehow
stood against the waves

-more more water metaphors lmao-

i'm prepared for a tidal wave
the tsunami that lies just at my feet
towering walls of water
ready to come down on me
i've always known it was coming
no hiding, or running, not this time
not anymore
no miracles, no rescue, no flying
i don't fear dying, because i've done this before
don't cry if i wind up as lifeless
a cold corpse up on the pacific shores
just remember that i went down fighting
and giving up wasn't my option anymore

-driving under the influence-

spinning tires and the smell of burnt rubber
shrieks and whirls of red and blue fill the air
i can't say i'm proud of what i've done
but in the end, i know it's fair
metal cuffed around my wrists
my mind is clouded, fogged, in a daze
you can't lie through your teeth with vodka on your breath
you must face the music
you must change your ways

-there's a monster under the bed-

although i tremble, i persevere
through the dreadful daylight
through pain and tears
my mind stays weary
my soul stays clear
through the wear and tear
of these endless years
i pursue my destiny
i overcome my fears

-Looking Back-

In the long summer hours of midnight
Living rapidly, as time burns like gasoline
I say to myself
"These are the nights that will flash before my eyes
In the moments before I fade into the light"
Staring up at the sky as my lungs search for breath
The chaos of the day behind me settles to utter silence
Breathing slows and my eyes settle on the stars
And my heart becomes calm, comatose
The next day ahead glows on the horizon
A new frontier of flashbacks I might collect
Until then, I live, as time keeps burning
So I soak up the gasoline
Until the end.

-hit me, it feels good-

i will always be stronger than the pain
i may be knocked down, but I'll live to see another day
because there are others who look up to me
people who love, and care, and live for me
i will go through it all for them
through broken bones and bleeding wounds
i will fight until the end

-a cold, dark night-

i couldn't tell you where my life is going
and frankly i wouldn't mind to forget
cause life keeps moving no matter what
but sometimes i wish we'd never met
after trudging through the empty night
snow falling effortlessly on my tired skin
i dug her out of the the side of the mountain
through the numbness, the loneliness, and freezing wind
through the violent night i worked, i sweat
just to uncover
my own regret
regret for trying, regret for the pain
when you try this hard for something gone
it's hard to not drive yourself insane
it's been four long years, and she hasn't left my mind
and yet it seems to her, i'm not worth her time
so now listen to me, please let the memories die
let our lives fade away, hope that we forget
because i dug you out of the mountain side
and repaid my debt

-more scat-

i'm a lover; i'm a fighter
sometimes a damsel in distress
i'm my own knight in shining armor
battling the demons of depression

Fate

At the end of it all- after the flame and fury of love,
after the unrelenting darkness that attempted to dismember you,
after traversing the clouded valleys of indecision,
and after empowerment, vigor, and revenge,
what is left to do, but rest on the mountain's edge
and ponder the path you've led.

-i miss being scared and afraid of the future-

calm cold nights by the fireside
aren't meant for reckless minds
for the destined are meant to live dangerously
my blessed curse, how fate makes me live this life
no, the snow does not fall softly on my skin
i get the freezing, empty, roaring winds
as i claw at frost and ice, gravel and rocks
frantically digging out the mountain side
so i might live to see another venturous night
i do not envy the presence of the former
for a calm still night by the fireside
that life just isn't mine
and to tell you the truth
i wouldn't want to live any other kind

This poem is for a friend of mine. We were headed to a bonfire up in the mountains where it was snowing heavily. We took a long path up the wrong road, and to make a long story short, I literally dug her suburban out of the snow- multiple times. At the end of the day the adventure was more fun to me than the fire was.

-If I died today, what would they say about me?-

My family would only have tears to spare
A violent loss of life, and family
It would destroy them
My closest family and friends,
They'd speak of my wildest encounters
Like driving recklessly on empty highways
Bumping to loud tunes with the windows down
The cool summer air on our faces
They'd speak of other things
Monumental movements of passion
Like the night three of us went on a hike
At midnight, up a dangerous peak
And somehow we made it to the top
To spend the night on top of the world
Marveling at the stars
Those not so close to me
Might say I was a troubled mind
Gaunt features resembling
A tired man, on the verge of death
And they might think,
"He pushed himself too hard"
and
"It was bound to happen sooner or later"
A troubled soul with one too many wrong turns
But always tried to swing back around
Catapulting myself into greatness
The likes of which I always under shot

What would I want them to say about me though?

Nothing.
I just want to be returned to the soil,
And the sea,
And the rocks,
And the trees.
To pass on in harmony
To have earned my peace

Who is it
That lit the first flame,
On the darkest night,
Of our final day?
Who is it
That committed a heinous sin-
As the destruction of our
humanity
Laid curse to all our kin.
What might become of us
As we walk blindly into
darkness?
Will we redeem our begotten
souls,
Or leave our redemption to the
tales of old?
What burdens shall we carry?
How many millennia will it
take?
Will we succumb to our
suffrage-
Or fulfill our forgotten fate?
They say it was long ago
That we crafted the glory of the
gods
Stripped souls built their
thrones
As we lay hollow, and broke
Dante traveled through the
echelons of the afterlife
And returned with tragic tales
of our irrefutable eternity
Whether we lay to waste in the
River Styx
Or exist solemnly in our
blissful ignorance
We conceived poetry, and
literature
The likes of which the world
had never seen
We told stories of prophets and
fiends
All to detail our enigmatic
intrigue
Unbeknownst to us we betrayed
ourselves
Separate stories became
seperate beliefs
Bearing swords, we wrought
bloodshed
Payment for prejudice,
collected by grief
We led crusades, and jihads
As death of men reeked in the
fields
Children were taught love, and
affection
Years later, we sent them
armed to the battlefields
Prophets practiced pedophilia
Politicians purged families for
power
The poor became mindless and
meek
The covetous grew stronger,
as they overpowered the weak
The tales of our dreaded destiny
disappeared
As our humanity crumbled
before us
Our dilapidated divinity was
lost to the ages
And heaven and hell, left
quietly at a cusp
Perhaps we should pray, just
one final time
And reach out to the heavens
For our humanity is dying.
Our beloved father, are't thou
still in heaven?
Might we still utter thy
hallowed name?
Might thy kingdom come-
And your will be done?
The forsaken are many
And the gates of hell are
unleashed
The oceans have turned to acid
And the earth crumbles beneath
our feet
Will you forgive us our lord?
For the sins we have made?
Are we still redeemable?
Or will we succumb to the
shade?
All remained quiet, as we
waited on his word
But the stories were stories, and
that's all they ever were.

-remembrance-

my mind is a mosh pit
bashed in and bruised
from all my painful memories
i tried to submerged them
from the surface
like a cerebral submarine
nevertheless, i tried my best
i just can't rid myself of feeling
i know what it's like
to walk alone through life
depressed, and numb, and freezing

.

                                        (some years later)

                                        it took sixty miles
                                        walking day and night
                                        before i wore down to the bone
                            weakness, and acceptance, and vulnerability
                                        became something i began to own
                                        the stars seemed so much brighter
                                        and the sun didn't seem to burn
                                        my feet felt so much lighter
                                        and i knew this peace, is what i earned
                                        from all the pain and sacrifice
                                        this lesson, i learned
                                        nothing is ever given in this world
                                        it is only ever earned
                                        we rise and fall and rise again
                                        and one day
                                        all will be returned

-peace and serenity-

i sit in front, on my grandfathers shop
where he collects and cuts his butchered meat

i patiently wait in the dusk of sunlight
soaking up the last droplets of summer heat
deep mountain woods grow with the darkness
as the scarlet sky turns to night
and the stars come out; and the crickets cry
i hold a rifle in my hand, but out of sight
my grandfathers cigarette smoke fills the air
cold steel laid softly, as i breathe as little as i can
tomorrow i'll be dreaming of this moment now
without any care, without any plans

-I Can't Sleep-

Fire burns a hole in the wall
Where the clock hung in my room
Now I stare through the void at night
And the looming threat of the moon

I'd tell you if I knew where the time went
Flames of memories begin to flicker
And now the ambers are fading away
I'll hand down the torch of life reluctantly

There's a ballad of silence in the air
Played by the sound of midnight wind
And this ancient house moving with me

Somehow the end of the world feels so close
When you're the only person you can see
Living and screaming, gasping for air

-What if?-

Infinite probability shows us that
Anything is a possibility
But this does not mean
Everything that can happen
Will happen in the span of time
Likewise infinity goes on for forever
Some infinities are larger than others
Like the infinity between
One to five
Is smaller than the infinity between
One to ten

-October-

Somewhere amidst these October skies
Autumn leaves descend to the ground
Where they will be trampled and left to rot

I wish I could write a beautiful song
But these October skies still block out the sun

Somewhere in the dead of night
My dauntless mind wanders this empty land
Searching for purpose and meaning under the sky
But I wonder if the purpose is lost in my mind

Even after the sun has risen, the trees remain dead
And all these thoughts can't break through the clouds
Scattered pieces cutting corners inside my head

When winter winds fill the city streets with frost
You can see my breath, in deaths final thoughts
Somewhere lost in the grains of time

Somewhere beyond this clouded sky
Is the golden light that seems to have died

-Antisocial-

I don't like people
I don't know what it is
I guess,
It's just the overwhelming anxiousness
That these people press on each other
Every goddamn day of their lives
Makes me want to blow my brains out...
They'd crawl on all fours, practically beg
Just to get an ounce of acceptance
Out of any old rotten stranger they meet
I've seen guys walk over glass
Just for a night out with a hot number
That couldn't explain to you
Why ice is cold or, the sky blue
I've met girls who'd break their heart
A thousand times
And still give that same rotten douchebag
Another chance
I don't know, I guess I'm not like that
I don't shun the awkward gaze you catch
Walking through a crowded street
I don't get that nervous attack
When the waiter tells you to enjoy your food
And you say "you too"
I don't care for societal norms
And I certainly don't care for cute potted plants
You neglect all winter as they wither and die
I don't know many things
And yet I think quite a lot
I don't say too much
So let me say this one thought
All I want to know is
Why do people search for truth?
When the only thing left to believe in
Is you?

-Drugs are Bad-

Sometimes I think about my brain
How it swells with a bit of nicotine
How it blurs with the shade of drunkenness
Sometimes I forget it's there
And when I forget it's there I forget I'm living
Up until my heart pounds with adrenaline
Aching for love, or for a fight
I forget I'm living until my knees buckle
As my lungs strain for air
After running from the cops
In the middle of the night
But these occasions are rare
I wish it would stay that way but
It never does and I go back
Stuck inside my head
Giving way to numbness
My false sense of reality
That thinks that I am me
And not a living being
I am capable of dying, and disease
Capable of wonderful and terrible things
Sometimes I forget what it's like
To remember
That I am me

80

-how to write-

to write is to live
and to live is to
go out and break the law
find yourself sleeping hopelessly
in a cold, lonely jail cell
and clean your puke up off the floor
when maggot infested bread
gags in your throat, still sore
from screaming at abusive prison guards
it also helps to fight a horrid war
to have shell shock, and post traumatic stress
to be surrounded with blood and gore
and to wake up every night
with growing anxiousness in your chest
because your wife can't recognize
the man she sent away anymore
and even then, if words cannot simply
pour out of your lips
and fill the pages like spilt ink
be meticulously observant, sit still, and think
look into the white veins of a budding leaf
how they look like it's own mother tree
and the roots beneath
feel something- feel anything
let your lonesome heartbreak over lost love
let anger foam at the corners of your lips
as you bark like a rabid dog
let sadness speak softly, but bleed deeply
like the slit wrists of a sorry suicide
but most of all, just stay alive
because living is pain
and through pain, you write

Welcome to the end of the book! I hope you've enjoyed reading. I'd like to offer this last poem as a piece of advice so you might write your own poetry. I hope that your poetry can be fulfilling, entertaining, and inspiring- as it has for me.

www.ingramcontent.com/pod-product-compliance
Lightning Source LLC
Chambersburg PA
CBHW021959290426
44108CB00012B/1134